Making... **Friendship BANDS**

Lynette Silver

illustrated by

Susie Poland

MILNER DODGEM BOOKS

First published in 1994 by
Sally Milner Publishing Pty Ltd
558 Darling Street
Rozelle NSNV 2039 Australia

Reprinted 1994, 1995 (3 times)

© Lynette Silver, 1994

Illustrations by Susie Poland
Design and typesetting by Shirley Peters
Photography by Benjamin Huie
Bands made by Vashti Silver
Printed in Hong Kong
National Library of Australia
Cataloguing-in-Publication data:

Silver, Lynette 1945.
    Making friendship bands.

    ISBN 1 86351 135 0

    1. Jewelry making. 2. Bracelets. 3. Anklets (Omaments).
    4. Friendship. I. Title. (Series: Milner craft series).

746.5942

Contents

For Vashti

What Are Friendship Bands?

Friendship bands or bracelets are brightly coloured cotton bands worn around the wrist and ankle. They originated in Central and South America and, although they are sometimes called 'Brazilian bands', they are not confined to Brazil. This traditional craft is practised in countries as far apart as Guatemala in the north to Chile in the south.

These attractive bracelets were discovered by international travellers, who then passed the technique and patterns on to others, so that the art of making the bands spread far beyond South and Central America. Today they are made throughout the world, and are given as a token of friendship.

Wearing Your Friendship Band

Some people believe that friendship bands will bring good luck to those who receive and wear them in friendship. According to legend, when the band is tied to the wrist or ankle a wish should be made by the person receiving it. This wish will be granted provided the band is not removed until it wears out and falls off. The moment the last thread gives way, the wish will be fulfilled.

Although the legend is fun, you will find that if you wear a band constantly it is difficult to keep clean. Surprisingly, leaving it on when bathing or showering does not help, as the cotton tends to become clogged with soap, making the colours dull. In time, with wear and being constantly wet and soapy, the fabric will begin to smell rather stale.

If you wish to wear your band while bathing, showering or when swimming in salt or chlorinated water, make sure that you rinse it well with clean water afterwards, then squeeze it as dry as possible with a towel.

How the Bands Are Made

At first glance they appear to be woven, but, in fact, friendship bands are made from a number of cotton threads which have been linked together with a series of simple knots. Since the only equipment you need are the threads and a large safety pin to anchor them, this is a craft you can do any time and in any place.

All bands are made by knotting one strand of thread around the thread next to it. Depending on the order in which the threads are used and the way in which the knots are tied, different patterns can be produced. If you have ever belonged to an organisation such as the Boy Scouts or Girl Guides, you will probably find that you are already familiar with the knots used. Don't worry if you are not – they are easy to learn and, after a bit of practice, you will be able to

work the design without referring to the instructions. By using your own colour combinations rather than the ones given in the patterns, you will be able to create distinctive bands that will be unlike any other.

It is usual to make friendship bands in pairs – one for the maker and one to be given as a gift to a friend.

What You Need

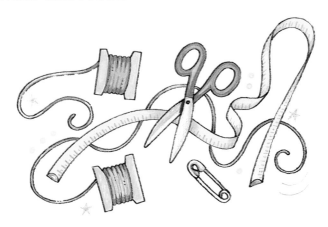

Thread

While it is possible to make friendship bands using any kind of cotton embroidery thread, for best results use a stranded thread such as the DMC stranded cotton used for the bands in this book. The multiple strands, which are not separated, help to give an interesting texture and the wide colour range allows you to experiment with hundreds of different colour combinations. Since embroidery cotton comes in loose hanks instead of being wound on reels, you might like to wind it around a broad strip of cardboard to stop it becoming tangled.

Safety Pin

The safety pin should be large enough to hold the threads and strong enough, when pinned to the anchor point, to provide the tension needed to keep the knots tight and even.

Anchor Point

Once the threads have been attached to the safety pin, the pin needs to be fastened to a suitable surface. You can easily provide such a surface by tying a large handkerchief or strip of fabric around the armrest or back of a chair, to the end of your bed or even to the handle of a door or cupboard. Provided that it is not covered in a material that may be damaged by pushing the point of the pin in and out, the padded arm of a chair or couch can be used, or the mattress on a bed. If you wish, you can even try attaching the pin to the fabric of your jeans just above the knee!

A pillow or cushion, which may slide about, is not really suitable as an anchor point as you need to hold the threads taut to get a good result. If the threads are not taut as you work, the knots will be loose and the finished band will be floppy.

Tape Measure

A tape measure or ruler is handy for measuring the strands. These should be cut in lengths of about 90 cm (1yd) for wrist bands or 1 metre (39") for ankle bands. If a tape measure is unavailable, you can always improvise. Stretch one arm out to the side, straight from your shoulder, and turn your head in the opposite direction. The distance from your fingertips to the end of your nose is about 90 cm (1yd). If you need the threads to measure 1 m (39"), add the length of your palm, which is about 10 cm (4"), to this measurement.

Scissors

You will need a pair of sharp scissors to cut the threads before you begin and to trim the ends after the band has been finished.

Choosing the Design

Unless you are experienced, it is best to begin with a simple pattern such as the Rainbow Design, which uses only one type of knot. It is also a good idea for beginners to use the colours suggested in the pattern. After a short while, when

you have a better idea of how the designs are built up, you will be able to choose your own colour combinations. When selecting colours, try to get a balance between light and dark shades as well as a contrast in the colours themselves. Bands that use too many light colours look pale and uninteresting. On the other hand, if you use only very dark shades, the design will not show up.

Preparing the Threads

1. Once you have chosen the pattern and the colours, cut the threads into lengths that are at least 90 cm (1yd) long for a wrist band and 1 m (39") long for an ankle band.

2. When they have been cut, hold them together in

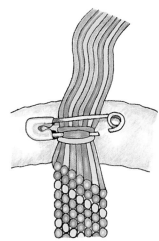

a bundle at one end, making sure that the ends are even. Using a single knot, tie the bundled threads to the straight bar of the safety pin, **leaving the first 15 cm (6") of thread hanging free.** These loose ends will be braided after the knotting has been completed.

3. Push the point of the pin into your anchor point and fasten it securely.
4. Sort the threads into the arrangement described in the pattern.

Tying the Knots

Friendship bands are made in exactly the same way as macramé. One thread forms the knot, while another is used as the knot bearer or the thread around which the knot is tied. When tying the knots it is important to hold the knot bearer taut and to use the tip of a fingernail to push each knot against the previous one. By keeping the tension tight and even, the rows of knots will be regular and the finished band will be very pleasing to the eye.

Knots

The half-hitch is the only knot you need to learn to make the designs that appear in this book. Simple to make, this knot will be familiar to anyone who has ever tied a horse to a hitching rail.

The first four designs use only double half-hitches. These knots, which are very strong and will not slip, can be made either anticlockwise or clockwise. It does not matter which hand you use to tie the knot or to hold the bearer thread taut, so use whichever is the most comfortable for you.

The final design in the book, the Criss-cross Design, is the most complex and uses a mixture of double half-hitches and combination single half-hitches. The instructions for tying the combination knots appear at the beginning of the instructior for the Criss-cross Design.

The Double Half-hitch *anticlockwise*

a. Place the threads in position.

b. Holding thread 2 taut with one hand, use the other hand to knot thread 1 around thread 2 in an anti-clockwise direction as shown in the diagram and then pull it tight. This is the first half-hitch.

c. Form a second half-hitch below it in exactly the same way. Pull the second knot tight against the first.

d. When the knot is complete, thread 1, which was on the left initially, should be on the right.

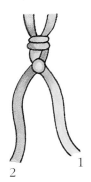

The Double Half-hitch *clockwise*

This is made in exactly the same as the previous knot, except it is made in the opposite direction.

a. Place the threads in position.

b. Holding thread 2 taut with one hand, use the other hand to knot thread 1 around thread 2 in a clockwise direction as shown in the diagram and then pull it tight. This is the first half-hitch.

c. Form a second half-hitch below it in exactly the same way. Pull the second knot tight against the first.

d. When the knot is complete, thread 1, which was on the right initially, should be on the left.

8

Finishing the Band

1. When the design has been completed, finish the band by dividing the threads into three even bundles and braiding them tightly in the same way as hair is braided into plaits. To prevent the braid unravelling, tie a temporary knot in the end. This braid will be used to make the knot to tie the ends of the band together, so it should be about one-third again longer than the braid at the other end. The length of the braids will depend on the size of the wrist or ankle it is to go around.

2. Undo the support knot from the safety pin, divide the threads into three bundles and braid them in the same way. Tie the band loosely around the wrist or ankle to check the length of the braids. Adjust them if necessary.

3. When you are satisfied with the length of the braids, tie a double knot firmly at the end of each. Trim the free ends to about 2 cm (³⁄₄").

To wear the band place it around the wrist or ankle so that the right side of the design is showing and tie the braids in a reef or flat knot, as shown below.

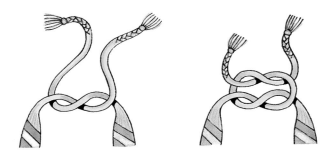

Caring for Your Friendship Bands

Your band will stay bright and clean for a very long time if they are washed before they become too grimy. Immerse the band in warm water to which you have added a few drops of liquid detergent or shampoo. Work the suds gently throught the band, rinse well in clean water and dry it flat, away from direct sunlight.

Rainbow Design

This band, which is made from seven different coloured threads using double half-hitches to anticlockwise, is the simplest design of all.

Threads

1 M (39") OF DMC STRANDED COTTON
IN EACH OF THE FOLLOWING
COLOURS:

RED (606)
ORANGE (971)
YELLOW (973)
DARK GREEN (700)
LIGHT GREEN (703)
DARK BLUE (824)
LIGHT BLUE (827)

Instructions

a. Cut the threads, and knot them to the pin.

b. Arrange threads so that (numbering from left to right) thread 1 is red, thread 2 is orange, thread 3 is yellow, thread 4 is dark green, thread 5 is light green, thread 6 is dark blue, thread 7 is light blue.

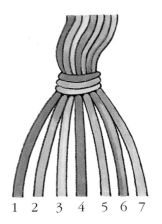

1 2 3 4 5 6 7

c. Using thread 1, make a double half-hitch anticlockwise on thread 2.

Do the same on thread 3.

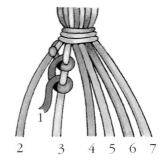

Do the same on thread 4.

Do the same on thread 5

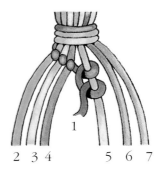

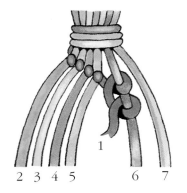

Do the same on thread 6.

Do the same on thread 7.

Thread 1 should now be on the right.

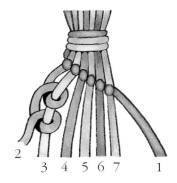

d. Using thread 2, make a double half-hitch anticlockwise on thread 3, then do the same on threads 4, 5, 6, 7 and 1. Thread 2 should now be on the right and you will have completed two rows of knots.

Continue knotting, using the method described in steps c and d above, always working from the left until the band is the desired length, ending with a light blue row.

Finish the band by braiding, knotting and then trimming the loose ends.

Water Snake Design

This pattern, which is worked in blocks using double half-hitches anticlockwise and then clockwise, was inspired by the graceful movement of the banded water snake.

Threads

5 X 1 M (39") OF DMC STRANDED COTTON IN PINK (601)

2 X 1 M (39") OF DMC STRANDED COTTON IN LIME GREEN (702).

Instructions

a. Cut the threads and tie them to the pin.

b. Arrange the threads so that (numbering from left to right) threads 1, 3, 5, 6 and 7 are pink and threads 2 and 4 are green.

c. For the first twist, using thread 6, make a double half-hitch anticlockwise on thread 7.

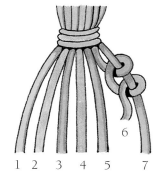

d. Using thread 5, make a double half-hitch anticlockwise on thread 7, then on thread 6.

1 2   3   4   7   6

e. Place the threads in position. Using thread 4, make a double half-hitch anticlockwise on thread 7, then on thread 6.

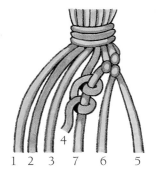

1 2 3 7   6   5

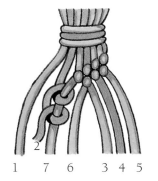

f. Place the threads in position. Using thread 3, make a double half-hitch anticlockwise on thread 7, then on thread 6.

1 2   7   6   4 5

g. Using thread 2, make a double half-hitch anticlockwise on thread 7, then on thread 6.

1   7   6   3 4 5

h. Using thread 1, make a double half-hitch anticlockwise on thread 7, then on thread 6.

i. Using thread 7, make a double half-hitch anticlockwise on thread 6. Arrange thread 7 so that it is on the right of thread 6.

The first twist is now complete.

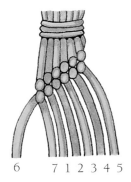

j. For the reverse twist, using thread 7, make a double half-hitch clockwise on thread 6.

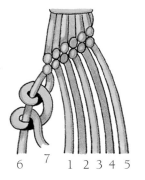

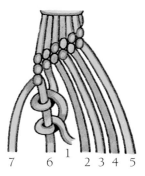

k. Using thread 1, make a double half-hitch clockwise on thread 6, then on thread 7.

l. Using thread 2, make a double half-hitch clockwise on thread 6, then on thread 7.

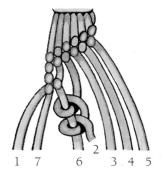

m. Using thread 3, make a double half-hitch clockwise on thread 6, then on thread 7.

n. Using thread 4, make a double half-hitch clockwise on thread 6, then on thread 7.

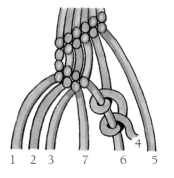

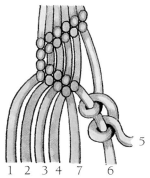

o. Using thread 5, make a double half-hitch clockwise on thread 6, then on thread 7.

p. Using thread 6, make a double half-hitch clockwise on thread 7.

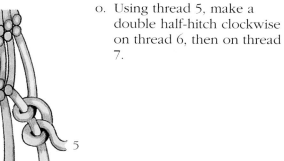

The reverse twist will now be complete.

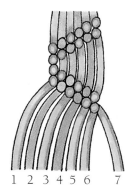

Continue making twists following steps c to p above until the band reaches the desired length.Finish the band by braiding, knotting and then trimming the loose ends.

Arrowhead Design

This band is made from four pairs of different coloured threads, using anticlockwise and clockwise double half-hitches to produce an arrowhead pattern.

Threads

2 X 1 M (39") DMC STRANDED COTTON IN EACH OF THE FOLLOWING COLOURS:

PURPLE (550)
DEEP LAVENDER (208)
LILAC (210)
BLACK (310)

Instructions

a.   Cut the threads and knot them to the pin.

b.   Arrange the threads so that (numbering from left to right) threads 1 and 8 are purple, 2 and 7 are deep lavender, 3 and 6 are lilac, 4 and 5 are black.

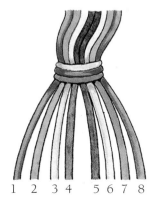

1   2   3 4   5 6 7 8

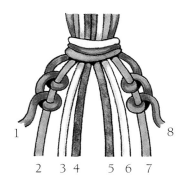

c. To work the first (purple) arrowhead, using thread 1, make a double half-hitch anticlockwise on thread 2. Then using thread 8, make a double half-hitch clockwise on thread 7.

d. Using thread 1, make a double half-hitch anticlockwise on thread 3, then using thread 8, make a double half-hitch clockwise on thread 6.

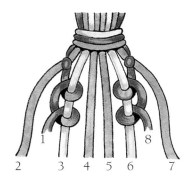

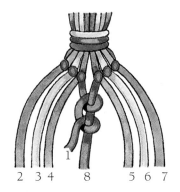

e. Using thread 1, make a double half-hitch anticlockwise on thread 4, then using thread 8, make a double half-hitch clockwise on thread 5.

f. Form the point of the arrowhead by using thread 1 to make a double half-hitch anticlockwise on thread 8.

19

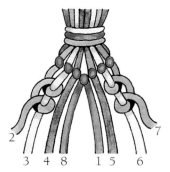

2   7

3   4   8   1   5   6

g. For the lavender arrowhead, using thread 2 make a double half-hitch anticlockwise on thread 3, then do the same on threads 4 and 8. Using thread 7, make a double half-hitch clockwise on thread 6, then on threads 5 and 1. Complete the arrowhead by using thread 2 to make a double half-hitch anticlockwise on thread 7.

h. Following the method described in step g, make first the lilac and then the black arrowheads. This will complete the first block of

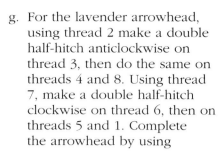

8   1

7   6   5   4   3   2

arrowheads. Continue in this way until five more blocks of arrowheads have been completed.

i. To work the centre of the design, using thread 1 make a double half-hitch anticlock-wise on thread 2. Then using thread 8, make a double half-hitch clockwise on thread 7.

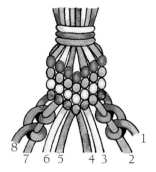

1   8

2   3   4   5   6   7

j. Using thread 1 make a double half-hitch clockwise on thread 2. Using thread 8 make a double half-hitch anticlockwise on thread 7.

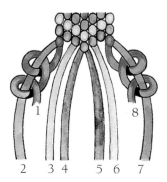

1   8

2   3   4   5   6   7

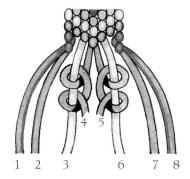

k. To begin the reversed arrowhead section, using thread 4 make a double half-hitch clockwise on thread 3, then do the same on threads 2 and 1. Using thread 5 make a double half-hitch anticlockwise on thread 6, then on threads 7 and 8.

l. To work the second reversed arrowhead, using thread 3, make a double half-hitch anticlockwise on thread 6.
Using thread 6 make a double half-hitch clockwise on thread 2, then do the same on threads 1 and 4. Using thread 3, make a double half-hitch anticlockwise on thread 7, then on threads 8 and 5.

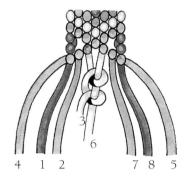

m. For the third reversed arrowhead, using thread 2, make a double half-hitch anticlockwise on thread 7. Using thread 7, make a double half-hitch clockwise on thread 1, then do the same on threads 4 and 6. Using thread 2, make a double half-hitch anticlockwise on thread 8, then threads 5 and 3.

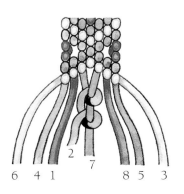

21

n. Following the method described in steps l or m above, make the fourth (purple) arrowhead. This will complete the first reverse arrowhead section. Continue in this fashion, always starting with the centre threads, until five more sections of arrowheads have been completed.

Finish the band by braiding, knotting and then trimming the loose ends.

Tropical Fish Design

Inspired by the brilliant colours of tropical fish, this design uses four different shades and is made from double half-hitches in a variation of the arrowhead formation.

Threads

2 x 1 M (39") OF DMC STRANDED
COTTON IN EACH OF THE FOLLOWING
COLOURS: ECRU
LIGHT GREEN (703)
DARK GREEN (700)
BLACK (310)

Instructions

a. Cut the threads and knot them to the pin.

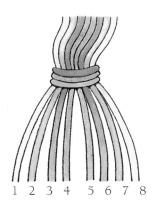

b. Arrange the threads so that (numbering from left to right) threads 1 and 8 are ecru, 2 and 7 are light green, 3 and 6 are dark green, 4 and 5 are black.

c. To work the fish tail, using thread 1, make a double half-hitch anticlockwise on thread 2, then do the same on threads 3 and 4. Using thread 8, make a double half-hitch clockwise on thread 7, then on threads 6 and 5.

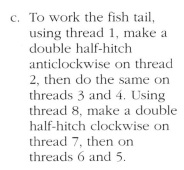

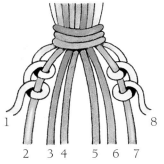

23

d. Using thread 1, make a double half-hitch anticlockwise on thread 8. The first arrowhead is now complete.

e. Following steps c and d above, make three more arrowheads, one using threads 2 and 7 (light green), one using threads 3 and 6 (dark green) and one using threads 4 and 5 (black).

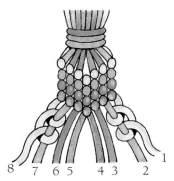

f. To shape the tail, using thread 8 make a double half-hitch anticlockwise and then one clockwise both on thread 7. Using thread 1 make a double half-hitch clockwise and then one anticlockwise on thread 2.

g. To shape the body of the fish, using thread 5, make a double half-hitch clockwise on thread 6, then do the same on threads 7 and 8. Using thread 4, make a double half-hitch anticlockwise on thread 3, then on threads 2 and 1.

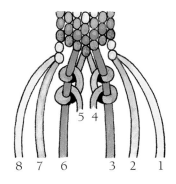

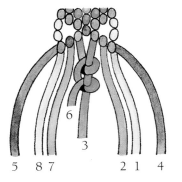

h. Using thread 6, make a double half-hitch anticlockwise on thread 3. Using thread 3, make a double half-hitch clockwise on thread 7 and then on thread 8. Then using thread 6, make a double half-hitch anticlockwise on thread 2 and then on thread 1.

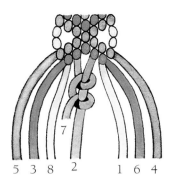

5 3 8   2   1 6 4

i. Using thread 7, make a
   double half-hitch
   anticlockwise on thread 2.
   Using thread 2, make a
   double half-hitch
   clockwise on thread 8.
   Using thread 7, make a
   double half-hitch
   anticlockwise on thread 1.

j. Using thread 8, make a
   double half-hitch
   anticlockwise on thread
   1.

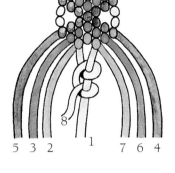

5 3 2   1   7 6 4

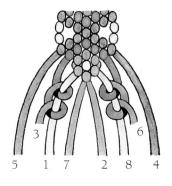

5 3 1   8 6 4

k. Using thread 2, make a
   double half-hitch
   anticlockwise on thread 1.
   Using thread 7, make a
   double half-hitch
   clockwise on thread 8.
   Using thread 2, make a
   double half-hitch
   anticlockwise on thread 7.

l. Using thread 3, make a
   double half-hitch
   anticlockwise on thread 1
   and then do the same on
   thread 7. Using thread 6,
   make a double half-hitch
   clockwise on thread 8 and
   then on thread 2. Using
   thread 3, make a double
   half-hitch anticlockwise on
   thread 6.

5   1 7   2 8   4

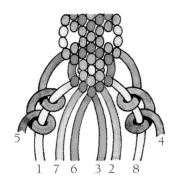

m. Using thread 5, make a double half-hitch anticlockwise on thread 1, then do the same on threads 7 and 6. Using thread 4, make a double half-hitch clockwise on thread 8, then on threads 2 and 3. Using thread 5, make a double half-hitch anticlockwise on thread 4. The fish shape is now complete.

Repeat steps c to m above four times. You will now have five fish on your band.

n. After the fifth fish, make three arrowheads, following steps c to e above for making the fish tail, but do not work the black arrowhead.

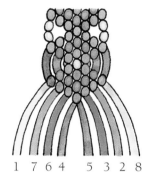

Finish the band by braiding, knotting and then trimming the loose ends.

Criss-cross Design

This six-colour design uses 12 threads and combines arrowheads and fish shapes to produce an eye-catching criss-cross pattern. Before you begin, you will need to master the anticlockwise and clockwise combination half-hitch knots. These two knots, which combine a half-hitch anticlockwise with a half-hitch clockwise, are not difficult, but they do require a change of hands halfway through the procedure.

Anticlockwise Combination Half-hitch

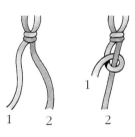

With this knot, the first half-hitch is worked anti-clockwise.

a. Place the threads in position.

b. Holding thread 2 taut in one hand, tie thread 1 in a half-hitch anticlock-wise. Pull the knot tight.

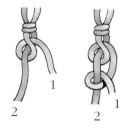

c. Pass thread 1 behind thread 2 so that it is on the right instead of the left. Change hands so that the hand that was holding thread 2 is now holding thread 1.

d. Holding thread 2 taut, tie thread 1 in a half-hitch clockwise. Pull the knot tight.

e. The knot is now complete. Thread 1, which was on the left in the beginning, has now returned to that position.

27

Clockwise Combination Half-hitch

With this knot, the first half-hitch is worked clockwise.

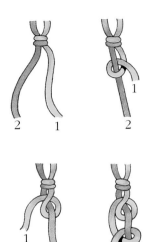

a. Place the threads in position.

b. Holding thread 2 taut with one hand, tie thread 1 in a half-hitch clockwise. Pull the knot tight.

c. Pass thread 1 behind thread 2 so that it is on the left instead of the right Change hands so that the hand that was holding thread 2 is now holding thread 1.

d. Holding thread 2 taut, tie thread 1 in a half-hitch anticlockwise. Pull the knot tight.

e. The knot is now complete. Thread 1, which was on the right in the beginning, has now returned to that position.

Threads

2 X 1 M (39") DMC STRANDED COTTON IN EACH OF THE FOLLOWING COLOURS:
LIME GREEN (702)
BRIGHT YELLOW (307)
PURPLE (550)
BRIGHT BLUE (995)
ORANGE (608)
HOT PINK (601).

Instructions

a. Cut the threads and knot them to the pin.

1 2 3 4 5 6 7 8 9₁₀¹¹₁₂

b. Arrange the threads so that (numbering from left to right) threads 1 and 12 are green, threads 2 and 11 are yellow, threads 3 and 10 are purple, threads 4 and 9 are blue, threads 5 and 8 are orange, threads 6 and 7 are pink.

c. To work the first arrowhead block, using thread 6, make a double half-hitch anticlockwise on thread 7. Then using thread 7, make a double half-hitch clockwise on thread 5, then do the same on threads 4, 3, 2 and 1. Using thread 6, make a double half-hitch anticlockwise on thread 8, then on threads 9, 10, 11 and 12. The first arrowhead is now complete.

1 2 3 4 5   7   8 9₁₀¹¹₁₂

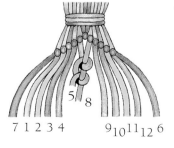

7 1 2 3 4   9₁₀¹¹₁₂ 6

d. Following step c above, use threads 5 and 8 (orange) to make the next arrowhead. Continue in this way to make another seven arrowheads. The last arrowhead, the ninth, will be blue.

29

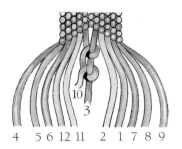

4 5 6 12 11 2 1 7 8 9

e. To work the criss-cross block, using thread 10, make a double half-hitch anticlockwise on thread 3. Using thread 3, make a double half-hitch clockwise on thread 11, followed by a clockwise combination half-hitch on thread 12. Using thread 10, make a double half-hitch anticlockwise on thread 2, followed by an anticlockwise combination half-hitch on thread 1.

f. Using thread 11 make a double half-hitch anticlockwise on thread 2.

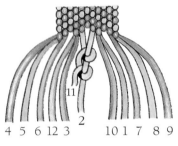

4 5 6 12 3   10 1 7 8 9

g. Using thread 3, make a double half-hitch anticlockwise on thread 2. Using thread 10, make a double half-hitch clockwise on thread 11. Using thread 3, make a double half-hitch anticlockwise on thread 10.

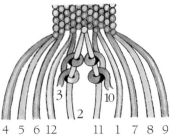

4 5 6 12   11 1 7 8 9

h. Using thread 6, make a double half-hitch anticlockwise on thread 12 and then do the same on thread 2. Using thread 7, make a double half-hitch clockwise on thread 1, then on thread 11.

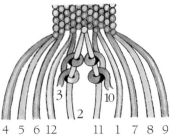

4 5   2 10 3 11   8 9

30

i. Using thread 5, make a double half-hitch anticlockwise on thread 12 and then on thread 2. Using thread 8, make a double half-hitch clockwise on thread 1, then on thread 11.

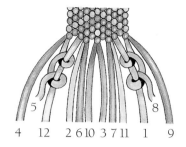

4   12   2 6 10 3 7 11   1   9

12   2 5 6 10   3 7   8 11   1

j. Using thread 4, make a double half-hitch anticlockwise on thread 12, then on thread 2. Using thread 9, make a double half-hitch clockwise on thread 1, then on thread 11.

k. Using thread 10, make a double half-hitch clockwise on thread 6, then on thread 5, followed by a clockwise combination half-hitch on thread 4. Using thread 3, make a double half-hitch anticlockwise on thread 7, then on thread 8, followed by an anticlockwise combination half-hitch on thread 9.

12 2 4 5 6   7 8 9 11 1

l. Using thread 6, make a double half-hitch anticlockwise on thread 7. Using thread 7, make a clockwise combination half-hitch on thread 5. Using thread 6, make an anticlockwise combination half-hitch on thread 8. Using thread 7, make a double half-hitch anticlockwise on thread 6.

12 2 4 10 5   8 3 9 11 1

31

12 2 4 5 6 7 8 9 11 1

m. Using thread 10, make a double half-hitch anticlockwise on thread 5, then on thread 6. Using thread 3, make a double half-hitch clockwise on thread 8, then on thread 7.

n. Using thread 12, make a double half-hitch anticlockwise on thread 2, then on threads 4, 5 and 6. Using thread 1, make a double half-hitch clockwise on thread 11, then on threads 9, 8 and 7.

12   2 4 5 6 3 10 7 8 9 11   1

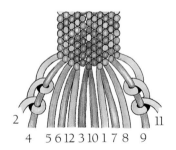

2   4 5 6 12 3 10 1 7 8 9   11

o. Using thread 2, make a double half-hitch anticlockwise on thread 4, then on threads 5 and 6. Using thread 11, make a double half-hitch clockwise on thread 9, then on threads 8 and 7.

p. Using thread 4, make a double half-hitch anticlockwise on thread 5, then on thread 6. Using thread 9, make a double half-hitch clockwise on thread 8, then on thread 7.

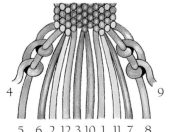

4   9

5 6 2 12 3 10 1 11 7 8

5   8

6   4 2 12 3 10 1 11 9   7

q. Using thread 5 make a double half-hitch anticlockwise on thread 6. Using thread 8, make a double half-hitch clockwise on thread 7.

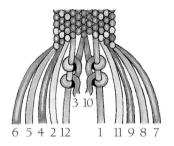

3 10

6 5 4 2 12   1 11 9 8 7

r. Using thread 3, make a double half-hitch clockwise on thread 12, then on threads 2 and 4, followed by a clockwise combination half-hitch on thread 5. Using thread 10, make a double half-hitch anticlockwise on thread 1, then on threads 11 and 9, followed by an anti-clockwise combination half-hitch on thread 8.

s. Using thread 12, make a double half-hitch anticlockwise on thread 1. Using thread 1, make a double half-hitch clockwise on thread 2, followed by a clockwise combination half-hitch on thread 4. Using thread 12, make a double half-hitch anticlockwise on thread 11, followed by an anti-clockwise combination half-hitch on thread 9.

12

1

6 5 3 4 2   11 9 10 8 7

t. Using thread 2, make a double half-hitch anticlockwise on thread 11.

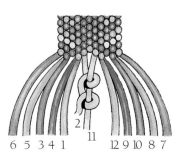

2

11

6 5 3 4 1   12 9 10 8 7

33

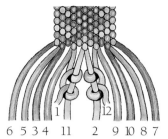

6 5 3 4　11　　2　9 10 8 7

u. Using thread 1, make a double half-hitch anticlockwise on thread 11. Using thread 12, make a double half-hitch clockwise on thread 2. Using thread 1, make a double half-hitch anticlockwise on thread 12.

v. Using thread 3, make a double half-hitch anticlockwise on thread 4, then on threads 11 and 12. Using thread 10, make a double half-hitch clockwise on thread 9, then on threads 2 and 1. Using thread 3, make a double half-hitch anticlockwise on thread 10.

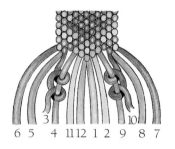

6 5　　4　11 12 1 2 9　8 7

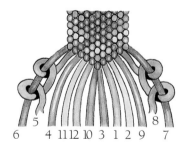

6　　4 11 12 10 3 1 2 9　7

w. Using thread 5, make a double half-hitch clockwise on thread 6. Using thread 8 make a double half-hitch anticlockwise on thread 7.

x. Using thread 4, make a double half-hitch clockwise on thread 6, then on thread 5. Using thread 9, make a double half-hitch anticlockwise on thread 7, then on thread 8.

5 6　　11 12 10 3 1 2　7　8

34

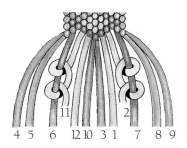

4 5 6 12 10 3 1 7 8 9

y. Using thread 11 make a
double half-hitch clockwise
on thread 6, then threads 5
and 4. Using thread 2, make
a double half-hitch
anticlockwise on thread 7,
then threads 8
and 9.

z. Using thread 12, make a
double half-hitch clockwise
on thread 6, then on threads
5, 4 and 11, followed by an
anticlockwise combination
half-hitch on thread 11.
Using thread 1, make a
double half-hitch
anticlockwise on thread 7,
then on threads 8, 9, and 2,
followed by a clockwise
combination half-hitch on
thread 2.

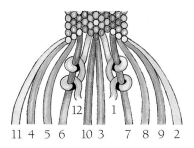

11 4 5 6   10 3   7 8 9 2

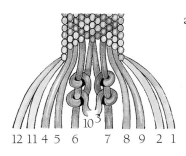

12 11 4 5 6   7 8 9 2 1

aa. Using thread 10, make a
double half-hitch clockwise
on thread 6, then on
threads 5 and 4. Using
thread 3, make a double
half-hitch anticlockwise on
thread 7, then on threads 8
and 9. This completes the
criss-cross and the first half
of the band.

bb. The second arrowhead and
criss-cross block are made
as follows. Using thread 6,
make a double half-hitch
anticlockwise on thread 7.
Using thread 7, make a
double half-hitch clockwise
on thread 5, then on
threads 4,10,11 and 12.

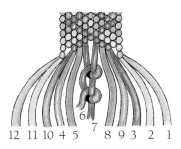

12 11 10 4 5   8 9 3 2 1

35

Using thread 6, make a double half-hitch anticlockwise on thread 8, then on threads 9, 3, 2 and 1. You will now have completed the first arrowhead in the second block.

cc. Beginning with threads 5 and 8 (orange) repeat the instructions for steps d to aa.

Complete the design by making nine arrowheads in the same order as the first block. Finish the band by braiding, knotting and then trimming the loose ends.